# *Lossland*

Luiza Flynn-Goodlett

Black Lawrence Press

Black Lawrence Press

Executive Editor: Diane Goettel
Book Cover Design: Zoe Norvell
Book Interior Design: Serena Solin

Copyright © Luiza Flynn-Goodlett 2027

ISBN: 9781625572288

All rights reserved. Except for brief quotations in critical articles or reviews, no part of this book may be reproduced in any manner without previous written permission from the publisher.
editors@blacklawrencepress.com

Published 2027 by Black Lawrence Press.
Printed in the United States.

Without in any way limiting the author's exclusive rights under copyright, any use of this publication to "train" generative artificial intelligence (AI) technologies to generate text is expressly prohibited. The author reserves all rights to license uses of this work for generative AI training and development of machine learning language models.

CONTENTS:


| | |
|---|---|
| We only talk in a one-sided | 1 |
| Let's play that game | 2 |
| It's enough to know | 3 |
| The past–weightless | 4 |
| My table's set with Tudor's | 5 |
| You lift the sunset's | 6 |
| One summer, camping | 7 |
| A telegraph won't do, | 8 |
| So I'll reach underground | 9 |
| In this dream: Your dog's | 10 |
| I guess we weren't made | 11 |
| Tomorrow I'll wake | 12 |
| Reflected in this | 13 |
| June ends, taking | 14 |
| My wife ducks a lifted | 15 |
| Yes, I chose to not see | 16 |
| Gone bad in ways I'd | 17 |
| All these irises piled | 18 |
| The garden blooms | 19 |
| Back in Prospect | 20 |
| It's Perseids season | 21 |
| In a dream, I bend | 22 |
| I return to our last | 23 |

Acknowledgments
Domestic Violence Resources

CONTENTS:

We only talk in a one-sided 1
Let's play that game 2
It's enough to know 3
The past—weightless 4
My table's set with Tudor's 5
You lift the sunset's 6
One summer, camping 7
A telegraph won't do, 8
So I'll reach underground 9
In this dream: Your dog's 10
I guess we weren't made 11
Tomorrow I'll wake 12
Reflected in this 13
June ends, taking 14
My wife ducks a lifted 15
Yes, I chose to not see 16
Gone bad in ways I'd 17
All these irises piled 18
The garden blooms 19
Back in Prospect 20
It's Perseids season 21
In a dream, I bend 22
I return to our last 23

Acknowledgments
Domestic Violence Resources

## AUTHOR'S NOTE

Someone I considered family disappeared into an abusive relationship. These poems begin six months after our last conversation.

We only talk in a one-sided
whisper: I bring, to our dark

room, irises that rose beside
my front steps after the first

rainy winter in a decade. You
offer silence again, so I hand

over the nest in my neighbor's
rhododendron, like the one we

watched hummingbirds build
last year before hatchings were

eaten by crows. I know, we're
not the only who lose. But I'm

slipping a note under the desk.
Promise not to read it aloud.

*[Turn to page 8 to set fingers on the planchet.]*
*[Snow glazes dark hair on page 20.]*
*[Dig up your childhood dog on page 10.]*

Let's play that game
where I'm a medium

and you're the ghost,
but you won't come

through, no matter
the gauze I swallow,

how I tap the table.
Why don't you hop

backward like those
jiangshi bodies you

were scared of as
a kid? I won't run—

beyond candle-glow
is your singular face.

*[Muddy feet on page 13.]*
*[Fall to your knees on page 18 among the petals.]*
*[Chew gristle from bone on page 5.]*

It's enough to know
we skate over each

other—water strider
and pond's surface—

you felt yesterday's
earthquake, woke

today. Enough are
camellias and pink

succulent flowers
that close at sunset.

You lift the camera
from your hip as oil

hisses in a wok. This
weaving grows under

my fingers—at first,
tapestry, now, tangle

of dark hair down your
back as you bike away.

*[Lose your footing on page 22.]*
*[Smell a huge, white flower on page 12.]*
*[Yellowjackets swarm toward page 7.]*

The past—weightless
as a marble—is all we

have. A predator got
to the hummingbird's

nest last night. She's
gone too, probably

killed with her chicks.
Of course, to die isn't

remarkable. We must,
eventually. What is—

finding each other,
even for a moment,

like marbles winking
across a vast expanse

of sand. My tiger's
eye, a twin of yours,

grows heavy with all
the love I can't pour

into your open palms
like so many marbles.

*[There's a spiderweb in your hair on page 15.]*
*[On page 9, hear a raptor call.]*
*[Cross the Hudson on page 18 riding a white bike.]*

It's enough to know
we skate over each

other—water strider
and pond's surface—

you felt yesterday's
earthquake, woke

today. Enough are
camellias and pink

succulent flowers
that close at sunset.

You lift the camera
from your hip as oil

hisses in a wok. This
weaving grows under

my fingers—at first,
tapestry, now, tangle

of dark hair down your
back as you bike away.

*[Lose your footing on page 22.]*
*[Smell a huge, white flower on page 12.]*
*[Yellowjackets swarm toward page 7.]*

The past—weightless
as a marble—is all we

have. A predator got
to the hummingbird's

nest last night. She's
gone too, probably

killed with her chicks.
Of course, to die isn't

remarkable. We must,
eventually. What is—

finding each other,
even for a moment,

like marbles winking
across a vast expanse

of sand. My tiger's
eye, a twin of yours,

grows heavy with all
the love I can't pour

into your open palms
like so many marbles.

*[There's a spiderweb in your hair on page 15.]*
*[On page 9, hear a raptor call.]*
*[Cross the Hudson on page 18 riding a white bike.]*

My table's set with Tudor's
biscuits, pickle-back slaw,

ribs that cling to the bone
because you like gnawing–

better than a Ouija board.
I know you've arrived when

the napkin stack dwindles.
I can't even remember our

last meal–another sunny
day, broken bread. I stare

down at an empty plate as
you, already full, stand up.

*[Sizzle garlic and ginger on page 3.]*
*[Make a trap on page 21 to hold all these wasps.]*
*[Hear a smash on page 16.]*

You lift the sunset's
caul over your hair,

red obscuring your
face. You're a giant

grouper pronged by
fishhooks, fox's path

of swaying grass, big
dipper rising, the gap

between every atom.
Your cottonmouths

flick in the shallows.
Startled by a jay's cry,

I don't feel joy, just
a momentary relief

from pain—the doctor
pauses, limb in hand,

knowing it must break
again before being set.

*[Your name is whispered on page 1.]*
*[The bees on page 19 are drunk on nectar.]*
*[Reach into the fountain of page 22.]*

One summer, camping
by a creek, we trapped

persistent yellowjackets
in a cardboard box with

a packing-tape window.
Before long, their churn

was all we heard. Though
today's box vibrates with

wingbeats, I won't chuck
it into the gulley and run,

will rip until wasps spill
out to cover me in sting.

*[Descend into a rush-hour subway on page 18.]*
*[Visit Tudor's Biscuit World on page 5.]*
*[Everyone clasps hands on page 14.]*

A telegraph won't do,
the passenger pigeon's

extinct, and I'm all out
of stamps. This worn

planchet stills under my
hands, the talking board

latched against a greater
silence. Only lift phone

from cradle, say, *Watson,*
*I want you. I need to see you.*

*[Page 22 is a bad dream.]*
*[Turn to page 16 to nick your thumb on broken glass.]*
*[Join the page-2 séance.]*

So I'll reach underground
to hoist matilija poppies

beside burr clover at your
feet. Remember being lost

on mushrooms at Prospect
Park, how a fountain roiled

with muddy arms? The dead,
though we weren't scared.

The pair of kites no longer
perches on my neighbor's

redwood, supplanted first
by a solitary peregrine, then

Cooper's hawk. Still, spring
brings its tumult–poppies

as big as dinner plates with
egg-yellow pistils for hearts.

*[Hummingbirds visit your dreams and page 4.]*
*[Page 20 dives in.]*
*[Slip off your shoes on page 14.]*

In this dream: Your dog's
back from the dead, fur

matted with mud. I open
your front door and hail

crests into a wave. Every
person I love surrounds

me, tugging at fishing lines
hooked into my flesh. You

step out of their circle and
back away with a line still

in your hand. Even dream
me knows what that means.

*[Go to page 2 if you're reading by candlelight.]*
*[Pocket a tiger's eye marble on page 23.]*
*[On page 17, break a silence.]*

So I'll reach underground
to hoist matilija poppies

beside burr clover at your
feet. Remember being lost

on mushrooms at Prospect
Park, how a fountain roiled

with muddy arms? The dead,
though we weren't scared.

The pair of kites no longer
perches on my neighbor's

redwood, supplanted first
by a solitary peregrine, then

Cooper's hawk. Still, spring
brings its tumult–poppies

as big as dinner plates with
egg-yellow pistils for hearts.

*[Hummingbirds visit your dreams and page 4.]*
*[Page 20 dives in.]*
*[Slip off your shoes on page 14.]*

In this dream: Your dog's
back from the dead, fur

matted with mud. I open
your front door and hail

crests into a wave. Every
person I love surrounds

me, tugging at fishing lines
hooked into my flesh. You

step out of their circle and
back away with a line still

in your hand. Even dream
me knows what that means.

*[Go to page 2 if you're reading by candlelight.]*
*[Pocket a tiger's eye marble on page 23.]*
*[On page 17, break a silence.]*

I guess we weren't made
of much—chains of days,

conversations, tuneless
voices in song. It took

so little to unhitch us.
It's natural to fall silent,

let the garden be overrun
by weeds. Still, as foxtails

tickle, I spy some orange
flashes of poppy, am sure

if I gave it the afternoon,
I could make us beautiful.

*[Laugh so hard you can barely breathe on page 15.]*
*[Step into the clearing of page 21.]*
*[Open to page 4 to play a belated game of marbles.]*

Tomorrow I'll wake
from dreams absent

of your voice to my
queen of the night–

grown from a cutting
of yours–in bloom,

and only think of its
scent filling the dark

house. I won't want
to tell you that they're

pollinated by moths,
and others that smell

of rotting flesh by flies.
So much is fashioned

from lack. But I won't
make a metaphor of it,

just cradle the flower in
my hand like a child's

head, grown heavy as
they nod off to sleep.

*[The frost on page 9 crunches underfoot.]*
*[Something is growing and green on page 17.]*
*[An angry buzz rises from page 7.]*

Reflected in this
stream, your face

is shattered and
then remade, but

the current rushes
on. Yes, minnows

hover, crayfish lift
claws below, but

such shimmering
light tires the eyes.

Memories must be
themselves only—

a TB-vaccine scar
dances on your

shoulder as you
slather oysters in

chipotle butter,
and I open wine,

the years rolling
over us like fog.

*[Someone on page 11 sings "Where Is My Mind."]*
*[Fling wildflower seeds onto page 17.]*
*[Skip a stone across the lake of page 19.]*

June ends, taking
the gloom along–

seances in candle-
lit rooms, breath

hitching at knocks,
memory piled into

mountains of shine.
I need only to back

away from this last,
best bet, not chart

another desire line
through your burr

clover, barefoot and
headless of the bees.

*[On page 1, gather armfuls of bearded irises.]*
*[Wander the streets of page 23.]*
*[Turn to page 6 if you were born bearing a caul.]*

My wife ducks a lifted
swatter to trap the huge,

metallic fly under a cup,
free it outside. I won't

pretend to harmlessness,
laugh too loud at some

inside joke we all once
shared, its origin already

forgotten. Arborists say
it's a sign when spiders

congregate at the tips
of branches where new

growth should be, and
this web twitches a reply.

*[On page 12, long-tongued bats drink nectar.]*
*[Turn to page 3 when you unravel.]*
*[Lift muddy arms toward page 11.]*

Yes, I chose to not see,
and when I did, to not

remember. *Lucky I'm tan,*
you said, *so you can't see*

*the bruises,* and the vase
of hydrangeas toppled,

shards scattering. It still
isn't safe to be barefoot.

*[Pull yourself up by the roots on page 20.]*
*[Uncork wine on page 13.]*
*[When snakes swim, hightail it to page 6.]*

Gone bad in ways I'd
never feared, things

are free to turn out
better than I hoped.

The long silence that
ends my monologue

might be coaxed into
bloom. Now picture

wildflowers I seeded
before winter rains

opening–each, a song
we both know by heart.

*[On page 8, lick stamp after stamp.]*
*[Fashion page 11 into a daisy chain.]*
*[Cry on page 23 until you can barely speak.]*

All these irises piled
at your feet are proof

of possibility—you can
still gather the crushed

petals of your life, ride
down Manhattan's long

spine, over a bridge, and
at the edge of the water,

camera slung around your
neck, text that you got out.

*[Turn to page 13 to show your scars.]*
*[Zombies chase you to page 2.]*
*[Open the buzzing box of page 7.]*

The garden blooms
foxglove, pendulous

angel's trumpets, and
bee-mobbed lupine–

poisonous, I know.
The scrying mirror's

blank face turned to
the sky, back resting

on white clover, we
pull weeds together.

Bees wobble, a little
drunk, over its surface

until the mirror stirs
with concentric rings.

You touch from below,
but I'll keep yanking up

this clover before yellow
flowers fruit to burrs.

*[When the earth shakes, open to page 3.]*
*[Falling stars streak down on page 21.]*
*[Be carried to bed on page 12.]*

Back in Prospect
Park, I should've

known, it wasn't
the dead. Living

was what we saw—
a frantic freestyle

through muddy
quicksand, our

heads never quite
surfacing. I've too

long trawled for
you—buffeted by

churning limbs—
and am no closer

to knowing ankle
from root. Marble

hardens around us
as the trees listen.

*[Grasp a gasping fish on page 10.]*
*[Your hands begin shaking on page 16.]*
*[Matilija poppies spring up on page 9.]*

It's Perseids season
again, when a great

darkness pours out
stars; though they're

imperceptible here in
the city, we counted

dozens once, craning
necks beside an old

logging road, the first
break we'd found in

the redwoods. Earlier,
we ripped cardboard

open to free a yellow
cloud of wasps, so we

wonder, can they see
all this light falling?

Do they even know
they've left the box?

*[If you've broken a limb, open to page 6.]*
*[On page 14, a sudden knocking.]*
*[When your stomach growls, open to page 5.]*

In a dream, I bend
over the fountain's

marble lip. Roiling
momentarily calms

and I can pick us out–
hair mud-caked, not

yet gray. *How could we*
*leave ourselves here?* I ask

before tipping forward,
reaching for your hand.

*[Dial a rotary phone on page 8.]*
*[On page 19, smell angel's trumpets at night.]*
*[Lift the flyswatter on page 15.]*

I return to our last
call, a sacred text,

until every word is
hand-illuminated:

You're scared, crying
so hard that strangers

stop to ask if you're
OK. I remember for

both of us now, bend
over sentences, catch

in your voice between
sobs, so when I stand

and walk into the rest
of my life, I carry truth's

marble, heavy in my
pocket, until returned.

*[On page 10, wake with a start.]*
*[Cradle an empty nest on page 4.]*
*[Open the note you were passed on page 1.]*

ACKNOWLEDGMENTS:

[You lift the sunset's] [So I'll reach underground] [It's enough to know], *Tupelo Quarterly*

[Reflected in this], *Hayden's Ferry Review*

[Tomorrow I'll wake] [It's Perseids season], *diode poetry journal*

DOMESTIC VIOLENCE RESOURCES:

**National Domestic Violence Hotline**

We are here to serve all those impacted by relationship abuse 24/7 confidentially. Due to high demand, you may experience longer wait times to connect with a live advocate. If you are unable to wait safely or aren't ready to call, chat or text—you can search our Directory of Local Providers section anytime for resources and support in your area.

- Hotline: 1-800-799-SAFE (7233)
- Website: https://www.thehotline.org/

**The Network/La Red**

The Network/La Red's 24-hour hotline provides confidential emotional support, information, referrals, safety planning, and crisis intervention for lesbian, gay, bisexual, queer and/or transgender (LGBTQ+) folks, as well as folks in kink and polyamorous communities who are being abused or have been abused by a partner. We also offer information and support to friends, family, or co-workers on the issue of domestic violence in LGBTQ+ communities. All hotline staff are trained in domestic violence, peer counseling, crisis intervention, and safety planning. You don't have to leave or want to leave your relationship to get support.

- Hotline: 617-742-4911 (voice) • 800-832-1901 (Toll-Free)
- Website: https://www.tnlr.org/en/

**CUAV (SF Bay Area)**

Founded in 1979, CUAV works to build the power of LGBTQ (lesbian, gay, bisexual, transgender, queer) communities to transform violence and oppression. We support the healing and leadership of those impacted by abuse and mobilize our broader communities to replace cycles of trauma with cycles of safety and liberation. As part of the larger social justice movement, CUAV works to create truly safe communities where everyone can thrive.

- Website: https://www.cuav.org/

PHOTO CREDIT: Tristan Crane

LUIZA FLYNN-GOODLETT (she/her) is the author of *Mud in Our Mouths* (Northwestern University Press, 2025) and *Look Alive* (Cowles Poetry Book Prize, Southeast Missouri State University Press, 2021), along with numerous chapbooks. Her poetry can be found in *Poetry Northwest*, *Ninth Letter*, *The Common*, and elsewhere. She serves as a poetry editor for the Whiting Award–winning LGBTQIA2S+ literary journal and press *Foglifter*. She was raised in the wilds of Tennessee and now lives in the SF Bay Area with her wife and rescue dog.

www.ingramcontent.com/pod-product-compliance
Lightning Source LLC
LaVergne TN
LVHW091545281026
851151LV00025B/269
*9781625572288*